Printed by
Printed Word Publishing
Hastings, East Sussex TN35 4NR

ISBN 978-1-9162602-7-6

Cover by Nick Daez

Content Ashlene Rosanne

Contents

MY HEART IS MY STRENGTH,

MY HEART IS
MY WEAKNESS

This book was born from a passion.

A passion that all humans should feel love for themselves. Hurt people hurt people and loved people love people.

HURT PEOPLE HURT PEOPLE AND LOVED PEOPLE LOVE PEOPLE

After years of working in the healing field, supporting people who were having difficulty loving and taking care of themselves, I decided to pen an honest account about healing from what I have learnt thus far.

We cannot be responsible for how others treat us. But we can be responsible for how we treat ourselves. True healing is when you take responsibility at a soul level to heal, to love, to accept and make peace with yourself. Ultimately begin to take actions in the present to fulfil the life you want. Information as to how to heal can be destructive without action on a soul level.

We are born into this world in a state of 'love and light' and we leave this world in the very same state of 'love and light'. Our light is divine, it is our birthright, and it is the one thing that cannot be taken from us. Whether we are born in our light or in the dark, our light is always available to us, just like the dark (difficult emotions) are also always available. There is such fear about the dark.

This fear creates a barrier to feeling these emotions and moving on from life's difficulties.

How people cope will vary, but until a feeling is accepted and acknowledged by you at a soul level then the process of healing cannot truly start. **No one else can process your emotions for you, and no one else can make true and meaningful changes in your life only you.** One step at a time in the direction of your heart can take you back into your light.

Never felt in your light? The light is there to be switched on by you for the very first time.

We humans are part of creation in this universe. The trees and plants are another part of creation, they face nature's storms whenever they come. They grow and they die. We as humans have no difficulty understanding the process of a plant's life. A humans life is the same, we live and then we die on this earth. Just like the life of a plant how well we tend to its basic needs determines how much it will flourish.

Regardless of the label you give yourself or the label that is put on you, you will always remain human. Labels are man-made and give the indication that life is stable (another man-made term) and there are definite outcomes. The only two definite in any lifetime; life and death.

Self-love is the foundation of life, self-love is taking care of and respecting your human makeup. The benefits of self-love are immeasurable, not only do they benefit you but also those around you.

Whatever you are healing from the essential ingredient is having the knowledge of your natural human makeup and taking action to look after that human makeup, even after difficult life experiences.

A lot of people are unaware as to how to love themselves and too often put themselves at the bottom of the queue for self-love and everyone else in front of them. If you do not know how to self-love, you will not be able to allow love in and you will not truly be able to give love out.

I remember wondering why one person seemed to suffer so much and another did not. What was the difference? I was aware that we were all just human beings born into families and cultures. Why did someone who is able to be kind, choose who was deserving of this kindness? Why is one person able to treat themselves with kindness while others struggle?

We are the creation that can communicate. In doing so we have complicated the human life experience. To such an extent that we are increasingly seeing people suffer with their mental health. We have allowed fellow humans to suffer over generations because of the man-made pollution that we are in some way different than our fellow human beings if they do not follow some man-made expectations or fulfil a label.

We as an individual have the power to harness our own inner peace, not to discover anyone else's peace or truth or decide when they heal.

Is this your time to heal?

Or are you preparing yourself to heal?

Whatever the reason.

Be kind to yourself.

The blame game. More man-made pollution that stops us growing and evolving.

If you have been hurt before which is highly likely, then it is also likely that you have hurt someone else whether you have intended to or not.

There is truth as to why some people are at an increased risk of mental health problems than others. However, this book turns all of this on its head and hands back to you, **your responsibility of looking after you. To unlearn old ways that are no longer serving your heart and focus more on the ones that do.**

We can inherit emotional baggage just like we inherit physical features. Just like you may have inherited your great great great great great grandad's nose, you may have also inherited his emotional baggage, difficult emotions that he did not express but rather stored in the mind. This is your subconscious, where the cells in your body remember. Thanks ancestors! We now know years gone by and still we are brushing difficult emotions under the carpet, we don't want to connect with painful emotions. But by not connecting with these emotions, they remain stored in the body, unable to find joy in the present or the future.

There are ways to bring these emotions to the surface, so that you can connect with pain and let it go, you do not need to know the origin of the emotion. With consistent physical and spiritual practice blocked energy centres will clear. With release of mental stress, physical health improves, cells are rebalancing, reprogramming free flowing energy, so that you are better able to manage daily emotions.

We are living in the never-ending story of life, the never-ending story of healing. Healing comes part and parcel with the human experience. The crap emotions are as real as the good emotions, let them all flow, soothe the crap ones and focus on the ones that bring you joy.

The mind is powerful, it can be powerfully destructive or powerfully powerful. Power sometimes can create fear in people, who have never known or felt their own power. Power is knowing your own self-worth. Power does not have to mean destruction, but it will mean destruction if you try and hold power over another.

There is a time to heal. It may take days or years for people to make peace with their inner pain, this is something that cannot be forced on someone.

Your mental health is the one thing that will not leave you, you will always feel emotions. The whole range of emotions, you can't pick and choose. We are all made up mentally and unless you are not human, you will encounter mental health problems in your lifetime.

Life will interrupt us all, there is no specific age for when life interrupts. From the day you are born to the day you die; life can potentially interrupt.

nati

INFORMATION

The natural human makeup is made up:
Physically
Spiritually
Mentally

We are unique human beings, with individual strengths and weaknesses.

We are aware now more than ever that despite the hierarchical systems set up within the world in years gone by to suppress and abuse, that we are all equal, and no human was or is deserving of such treatment. With this knowledge embedded now in equality legislation, there is an overwhelming sense of anger within the world as to why it ever happened. Anger is a real emotion but not released in a safe and nurturing space, can cause more destruction in your life.

RESPONSIBILITY

Given that we have access to so much information is fantastic, we know so much about the potential impact of certain life experiences, the impact of certain diseases, the impact of labels, the impact of suppressive systems.

Information helps us to make sense of why we feel the way we do, reflect on, learn and grow from the good and the bad life experiences. Life experiences will change our emotions, in any given moment.

The feeling when you are going through dark times in life can feel like forever, its hard to feel where to turn or what to do. Sometimes we turn to others for support, sometimes we blame others for not helping enough.

What are you doing to help yourself?

Take responsibility for how you feel.

Taking responsibility for your life is the starting point of life, we can do this at any age when we decide to create our own story. To not hold others or a man-made label responsible for our lives.

We are privileged in this part of the world with free healthcare; physical, mental and spiritual services.

But with this privilege, comes a feeling of entitlement. Yes we are entitled to a system we ultimately fund. That is the man-made law around the system.

We want to be 'fixed' spiritually, mentally, and physically when we are needing it. If we do not get it, then there's uproar.

The human body is made up with physical and spiritual energy.

NEITHER ENERGY MORE SUPERIOR. BOTH ENERGIES REQUIRED TO GIVE BALANCE TO THIS EARTH. THE EARTH IS MADE UP PHYSICALLY AND SPIRITUALLY.

Nurturing both energies will bring about balance to the mind, body, and spirit. Your energy system vibrates out into the universe – like a 'soul' language. Your physical and spiritual practice will write the soul language. Feed your energy well and it will talk well 'intuition'. Your thinking will become less clouded, your purpose that brings you joy will be clearer.

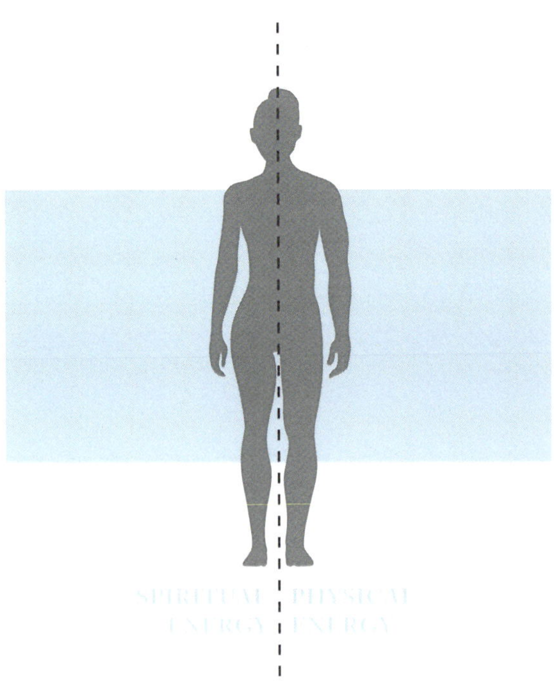

The physically strong builder cannot build all the houses, nor does the house owners want the same builder. The same works with spiritually strong people. **The people that need you will come to you**. Bear in mind the builder gets paid for their services (there is an energy exchange a sign of respect for their work), what are you being paid? Be mindful of energy exchange.

Spiritually strong people are lightworkers and physically strong people are lightworkers. Anyone creating a life they love that makes their heart swell is a lightworker in this world, they are standing in their truth.

STANDING IN YOUR TRUTH, IS A PHYSICAL AND SPIRITUAL PRACTICE OF A LIFETIME.

This is the information, and without you taking action on a soul level, you might as well be dreaming. The reality is that **you** have to take the action.

Human relationships come and go, we learn and grow. In the current world of technology, family, friendship/work relationships are almost constant, there is no space. We are constantly aware of what's going on in so many other people's lives.

How much is this adding to yours? How much of this is ensuring that you are following and listening to the direction of your heart? How much of this is ensuring that you are spending time with the people you love and the people who love you?

THE PHYSICAL BODY

THE PHYSICAL BO

THE PHYSICA BODY

What are you eating and drinking?

What physical exercise are you doing with your body?

This will have a knock-on effect on your health.

SPIRITUAL BODY

Spirituality is a practice of gratitude to the source.

What gratitude are you practicing to the source?

This will have a knock-on effect on your health.

Source to many has different names. Practicing gratitude to the source is somewhere where you should feel free from external influence, to just be you.

Regardless of if you have a name for source or not, spirit is inbuilt within us.

How you practice your physical and spiritual health is for you alone to decide.

By attending or being part of a spirituality practice does not mean you are practicing spirituality.

In the same way it can't be assumed that being a member of a local doctor's surgery you are taking care of your physical health. Likewise how you won't get physically fit by eating healthy once in a while; spiritual health works exactly the same. It's a practice of a lifetime.

To benefit from both physical and spiritual well-being, you must practice both on a soul level. No one can practice this for you.

MENTAL HEALTH

Life will happen to us all, the good and the bad are inevitable in creation.

In the fast pace of the world we live in, no one wants the crap feelings because they get in the way so to speak.

So we mask these feelings up only to create more difficulties.

Crap feelings need listened to and processed by you. The more layers of unprocessed emotions, the more inner energetic weight we carry. Which can result in poor coping mechanisms like addiction, control issues and abuse. The more you resist emotions, the more strain you place on the body creating stress. Stress is normal but it is when it becomes chronic that stress will impact the body, mind, and spirit. Thankfully we have a world full of amazing people that can support you with releasing difficult emotions, until you are able to make it through the dark back home into your light, your truth.

When you suffer from poor mental health and are stuck in an emotion, you are stuck with direction. The direction back to your light, to your truth. Traumatic, difficult life experiences can change the direction you want to take in life.

The word 'stability' has a lot to answer for. We want x, y & z, and then we acquire all we want for that 'stable life'….and we are not happy…why not? Because life is life. Just like the bills keep coming in life so do our emotions, the whole range from good to bad.

No matter what you acquire in life, there is no free pass to just having the good feelings.

MENTAL
WEIGHT
SELF LOVE
PRACTICE

Acti

ACTION

Humanity before us knew at a soul level that the enforced control and abuse over them was wrong. They fought against this, fighting with the information solely from their heart. We have the information now, handed to us that we humans are equal.

Human equality is now thankfully embedded in legislation within a lot of countries, but not all as yet.

Actions on a soul level will continue to speak louder than words on paper. We must continue this work into our light, by actioning, looking after and respecting our human makeup.

THE POWER OF YOUR 5 SENSES

The simpler the better.

The senses used in nature have the ability to clear the noise. Giving you the ability to feel your emotions without influence.

The natural environment is the most nurturing environment for any animal. Humans are no exception. With the increase in technology, we have increasingly polluted our senses with the lack of true space in our lives.

Think of reconnecting, recharging with earth, the natural environment. Children and adults are not always ready to talk through their emotions. There is so much emphasis on verbal expression, but there are other areas to consider if verbal expression is not your strength. This will come in your own time.

The power of the 5 senses used in nature will top up your self-love.

SMELL

SIGHT

HEARING

TOUCH

TASTE

DO THEY ALL BRING YOU JOY PRESENTLY?

HUMAN CONNECTION

In life too often we only realise the significance of human connection when faced with death of someone you love.

Love never dies.

But that physical connection does.

The importance of spending physical time with the people you love is another practice of self-love.

Who is important to you?

Who's hand will you be holding in the end?

PHYSICAL PRACTICE?

SPIRITUAL PRACTICE?

The more you complicate the inner practice of self-love, the more you complicate your outer life experience.

BASIC ACTIONS TO TOP UP SELF-LOVE

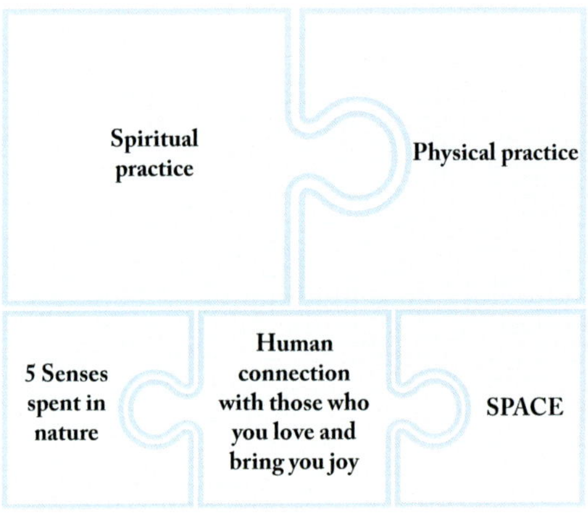

CHOICE

It is your choice to action the information.

We are living breathing power houses. Made up of a flow of energy. How we fuel our powerhouse is our choice.

WHAT IS YOUR FOCUS?

Any focus that is not born from love in your life will interrupt your natural state.

Starve any destructive distraction.

HUMOUR

Having fun in life, doing what brings you joy builds resilience.

SPACE

Space provides time to reflect, to move forward with love and make choices that are true to your heart.

Because we are all human and we will be in the light and in the dark at different stages of life. When you are in the light some people will be in the dark, and vice versa.

The truth is both exist - light and dark.

It does not matter the human relationship with a person, be that a family member, work colleague, friend, you cannot pick when they are in the light or dark of life. Just like they cannot pick when you are in the light or dark of life.

HUMAN JUDGEMENT

It is a natural emotion.

That was born from a man-made belief system as to how a person should be.

You will judge others.

You will judge yourself.

They will judge you.

They are not you.

You are not them.

Spiritually strong want all to be spiritually strong.

Physically strong want all to be physically strong.

Truth is we need balance on this earth. The earth is made up physically and spiritually. Use your strength to do what you can for humanity.

nclus

CONCLUSION

I am human.
I am my physical and spiritual practice of a lifetime.
I am my truth.
I am love.
I am light.

Choice is a strong word when you are healing, as you can't see the wood for the trees. But so is honesty a strong word. Our world is loosing its truth in the face of honesty. Why can't we be honest with the facts? Because of the potential impact. So far the impact of increasing services to support, has meant there is a need for further increase in support, creating dependency. We all need support of that there is no doubt, but at the same time you need to be taking action on a soul/ individual level with your physical and spiritual practice to benefit from this support. Again, information without action on an individual basis can be destructive.

Life goes on after we learn how to heal our difficult past or inherited emotions, ups and downs still come and go.

The space in this book is on purpose.

Reflecting the importance for space in your life.

Space is an art, in this 24/7 accessible world.

Space to give you time to accept the way you have previously felt and currently feel. No one can feel your feelings. No one can tell you how you feel. Equally you cannot tell anyone how they should feel, regardless of your relationship with that person. Listen to your body in a safe space. Given we are so heavily influenced by outside noise it's hard to know what you feel, but with continuous spiritual and physical practice, you will know, you will know by the feeling.

On one hand technology has brought so much destruction to the world as it was before, when people were more physically and spiritually active. On the other hand, people are now aware that we are all humans, all equal. With new knowledge, comes new ways. Our physical and spiritual practice are as important as they always were in our health.

In truth who you are is an ever-evolving story whilst on this earth. The only truth I have come to know is that we enter this world in a state of 'love and peace' and this is the state we leave. 'Love and peace' are our natural state, thus love is our foundation to life. Fueling your life with anything of the contrary will disturb your peace.

Whilst being mindful that because we are part of creation means that storms will come our way, happiness will come our way too. For some, unfortunately early in life they are born into storms, know nothing other than storms, thus the inherited cycle repeats for them.

The magic is that the universe, the natural laws do not judge and are ready and waiting when you are to turn on your light, even if it is for the first time.

About the author:

Ashlene Rosanne was a social worker and group facilitator for a mental health charity before recognising that talking therapies alone without physical and spiritual practice on an individual level often nurture an issue and do not always enable the person to move on from past pain. Currently working as Reflexologist, Reiki Healer and Meditation teacher.

This book 'Truth Who Am I' is written in simple terms on purpose, so that all ages can hopefully benefit from it, regardless of age or academic ability. Everyone deserves the chance to heal. I very much felt at the time of writing that I had learned a lot over the years (however every day is still a school day and life often reminds me of this one) and that passing this information on would hopefully benefit others.

Whether you are someone who is struggling to move forward in life and do more of what brings you joy or if you're a parent/carer for someone who is struggling with direction in life, I hope that you get some inspiration or comfort from this book.

Perfection is you in action, and that comes with trials and errors.

The book is simply written, the message in the book remains simply powerful for the soul. The cover of the book was painted by Nick Daez, a Yoga Teacher and artist based in the Philippines.